CONTENTS

Acknowledgements

I would like to thank Sally McKeown for her advice and for getting me organised, and Earlsdon Writers for their constant support and encouragement.

Coming in From the Snow

When I came in from the snow
Across the park out of town
You stared at me
Standing
Blue wellies
Green parka
Red woolly hat.
You stared at
My carrier bag
HMV Records
And said
You've never been
Into HMV
Looking like that
You might have been seen
By one of my friends.

And I was with you
Black crombie
Doc Martens
Close shaved head.
I walked beside your
Jeans more holes
Than patches.
At your Grandfather's
70th birthday party
For all the relations
I danced with you
And your feather earring.

So I was glad
You were there
When I came in
From the snow.

Break Down

Is there always a rapist

When in the early hours

Her car breaks down

And she pulls on to the hard

Shoulder to cry on

Or was it her bad luck

That two men wanting a fuck

Were on a have it away day

On that particular motorway

And did they feel disgust

At their lust

And vow never again

Yet live forever in her brain.

Calling All Women

This weekend

Let's bend

the rules

and spend

the hours

pretending

we're the

stronger sex.

Let's cruise

the motorways

in twos

searching out

the stranded

lone male

motorist.

Let's pretend

to be

his friend

to lend

a hand

to mend...

or menace

for revenge.

Just As

Just as

The young people

Leave

Leasing me

Back to myself

Again

Freeing spaces

Outside and in

The old people

Begin

To occupy

The edges

And I fall

Back

Into the loving trap.

That Box of Chocolates

The box of chocolates that you sent,
I know that it was kindly meant
But to resist requires a lot
Of willpower which I have not got.

Safely wrapped in cellophane
And hidden on the highest shelf
A box is safe for several days
Until I have to tempt myself

Once the cellophane's undone
I tell myself I'll just have one
But one alone is not enough
I catch the taste and start to stuff

Chocolate fudge, montelimar
Hard centres, but my favourites are
The caramel and creamy coffee
Hazel nut and liquid toffee

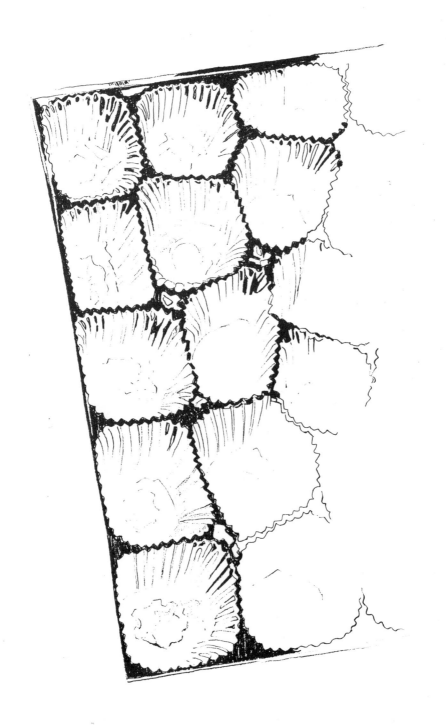

The strawberry creams are not for me

They're far too sweet and sickly

But when they're the only ones left in the box

Even they disappear very quickly

I know that carrot sticks are crunchy

That celery is very munchy

Radishes are lovely too

But chocolate is bad for you

So next time when you want to say

Thank you for a lovely day

Please can you think of something that

Won't add to all my layers of fat

A book, some scent, a bottle of wine

Or a bunch of flowers would be just fine!

The Obstetrician

I would like to make
a constipated obstetrician
lie flat on his back
strapped to a slab
exposed in his shirt
I would bend up his legs
and say
push
come on
bear down
push

And when he said
wouldn't squatting
be more natural?
I would ruffle his hair
tell him to be a good boy
smile a superior smile
and say
hush
we know best
now come along
push
push
push out all this
bullshitting.

12

Granite Pebble on the Shelf

In my hand you are smooth cool

My thumb nestles gently in your curves

You are hard and strong

Yet how out of place

Carried by chance

Foreign in this room.

Do you miss the sea's roar

Slaking over you, ice cold?

Do you miss the warm sand

Nuzzling your grey body?

Away from the tossing waves

Becalmed on this shelf

You will remain undiminished

Unchanged over time

Do you mind about that?

The Family Tree

In Harrod's window, trees created
Gold and red sophisticated.
To perfection decorated

New shining baubles for our tree
Gold and red, I could just see
How beautiful our tree would be

Now here it stands; my creation
Decorated to perfection
The ideal Christmas colour scheme
Red and gold on darkest green

Then they came in and made a fuss
They didn't like it. It wasn't "us"

Where was the angel with the wobbly head
That Charlotte made in nursery school
You can't leave her off the top, they said

They brought down the box from under our bed

Here's Paul's Father Christmas made from toilet rolls

He usually goes about here, they said

Then Adam found his Holy Ghost

I think he really means Heavenly Host

It's a tinsel cross in silver and red

I'll put it right at the front, he said

Then I looked into the box and found

My man in the moon with his face so round

The golden house, and the silver bell

The little blue bird, my pale pink shell

We hung them all on the tree as well

What had become of my perfect creation

The Christmas tree of sophistication

My colour scheme of gold and red

It looks much better now, they said.

The Blackbirds

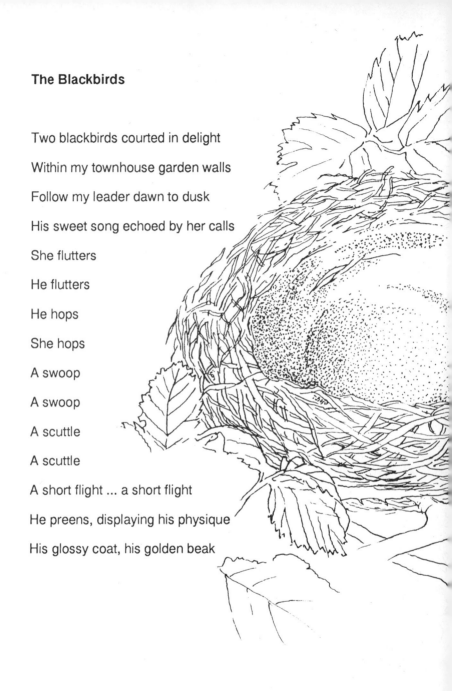

Two blackbirds courted in delight

Within my townhouse garden walls

Follow my leader dawn to dusk

His sweet song echoed by her calls

She flutters

He flutters

He hops

She hops

A swoop

A swoop

A scuttle

A scuttle

A short flight ... a short flight

He preens, displaying his physique

His glossy coat, his golden beak

But yesterday he came alone

He sang and sang

She did not come

Has she flown off, the flighty piece

To build a nest with some bird else?

Is she in some deep disgrace

To keep her from her favoured place?

Or is she lying dead alone

Far from him

And cannot come?

Today his dusty feathers fall

He calls no more upon the wall

He simply stands with yellow gape

Mourning the absence of his mate

The Christmas Tree

they came with blades

the noise of saws

shearing the forest

stillness.

culling young trees

to stand in corners

hung with brilliance

reflected

in the gaze of babes.

not those same babes

stabbed by swift knives

murdered

in their innocence

a slow death for the tree

immured in four walls

shedding

its painful pine

cast out naked

on the twelth day.

Encounter with a Pre-Raphaelite

From her portrait

Swathed in silken folds

Dark tresses tumbling

One arm resting on marble

The slender girl

Beckons my mortality.

"Death is forever"

She stabs my mind

Provoking silent screams.

It's not the dying.

It's the not being.

No me on earth.

It will all go on

Without me.

It's all going

Too quickly.

I want another turn.

Is it only me?

No says the damsel in the landscape

I'm screaming too.

Woman Weeping

She sat there remembering
The brilliant dawning
The small bright torch
On the threshold shining

Enticed by a golden ring
The gift of a young prince
She sought his protecting
Too carefully moving

Mothering consuming
Other flames burning
Her fingers protecting
From the light shielding

Now in her late years
Remembers the shining
Weeps
In the dim light remaining

Death in Hospital

death images:
curtains
a darkened room
silence.

so why are you here
in this bright ward
haunted by old girls
calling confusion

Coronation Street in the corner

where brisk blue nurses
are changing sheets
that smell of mortality

not the death images
you had imagined as
slowly
slowly
in full view
you suck in
your last breath
your last breath

Cracks

such beautiful wallpaper
a perfect covering
for cracks in the plaster
finer than spiders' webs

such a beautiful couple
a perfect relationship
the cracks carefully
papered by smiles

peeling wallpaper reveals
plaster shattered
like dropped pastry
exposing
structural damage

The Empty House

The house is quiet, still

They've all gone out at last

She wanders through each room

Picking up their droppings

Folding and restoring

Till all is calm and neat

The hours ahead are hers

Silence settles soothing

The empty rooms embrace

She sits with her own thoughts

Without guilt she reads

Her book, and falls asleep

Wasting her solitude

In dreams.

In the Heat of the Moment

I'm in Tesco's

by the bread

and the heat

begins to spread

from my feet

up to my head

on fire

perspire

I'm wet

with sweat

oh no

not yet

just let

me get

out there

fresh air

or tear

off shirt

stand there

in underwear

or bare

then blush

hot flush

For A Friend

You say the test

Was positive

And ask for a poem

Positive

And your eyes

Shocked wide

With held back tears

Your decorated eyes

Positive

And your fear

Catches me

Positive

Your sexy voice

A lump in your breast

Positive you say

Trapped

Malignant

You ask for a poem

There must be words

words to comfort

words to warm

to melt

to mop up

icy fear

words to smooth

to soothe

the bruising

anger

words to bless

caress

enfold

and hold

and hold

there must be words

there will be words

words to lighten

to brighten

often to soften

ever after

making laughter

Talk

he talked

she listened

he talked about himself

she listened to him

talking about himself

he talked until

he satisfied himself

she listened to

his satisfaction

she

could not speak

his ears

were waxed

with self

she sat

silently tasting

the blood

from her bitten lips.

Loreta, aged 24,

Died Vilnius, Saturday January 12th 1991

On the dark hillside the people are waiting
Defending the huge concrete media tower
Transmitting their plight to the rest of the world.
Alone by her campfire Loreta is praying
Through distant darkness she hears tanks approaching
In bitter cold she prays for her land.
The Soviet tanks are climbing the hillside
Advancing relentlessly clearing a trackway
Ploughing through hedges and tearing the ground.
As they loom nearer, one pauses, rolls backwards
Loreta runs shouting, "You fascists ... Lithuania"
A few fractured flowers wave in her hand.
The tank lunges forwards then moving so slowly
Crushes her young body into the ground
The flowers she carries fly up before her
Falling to rest in the eye of the tank.

No Rehearsal This

No rehearsal this, for other lives.

With life, like parts, prepared and our mistakes

Cancelled out to start again. Oh no.

This is your only chance, so choose with care

And treasure every age. For soon your time

Upon the stage will cease and you will be

As dead as ashes after burning leaves.

Your eternity will lie with friends

And small resemblances in future kin

Not in some unfound heaven up above.

Life will go on without you. You have had

Your turn. No action replays are allowed.

So scream your silent death fears if you must

Your final part will be as of the dust.